History's Big Mistakes

Adam Bowett

Illustrated by Chris Mould

 Belitha Press

First published in Great Britain in 1994 by
Belitha Press Limited
London House, Great Eastern Wharf,
Parkgate Road, London SW11 4NQ

ISBN 1 85561 588 6

British Library Cataloguing in
Publication Data
CIP Data for this book is available from
the British Library
Editor: Carol Watson
Art Director: Frances McKay
Consultant: James Walvin

Printed in Hong Kong

CONTENTS

INTRODUCTION

What is history? History is a record of past events. It just happens, and most of it seems to happen whether we want it to or not. Some people find this upsetting, since they like to be in control of things. They think that if something doesn't happen the way they planned it, then it is a mistake.

Some mistakes, like the sale of Alaska, turn out well. Others, like the building of the battleship *Vasa,* not so well. One man's mistake is often another's good luck. The episode of the Trojan Horse was disastrous for the Trojans, but very lucky for the Greeks. Bach was turned down as an organist by Hamburg but at Leipzig he composed most of his best work. If Columbus had not discovered America by mistake, there would be no hot dogs in the world!

Mistakes are like life – it depends on how you look at them. Some mistakes are funny, some tragic, but all have something to tell us about our world and its history.

Words in the text in **bold** are explained in the glossary on page 31.

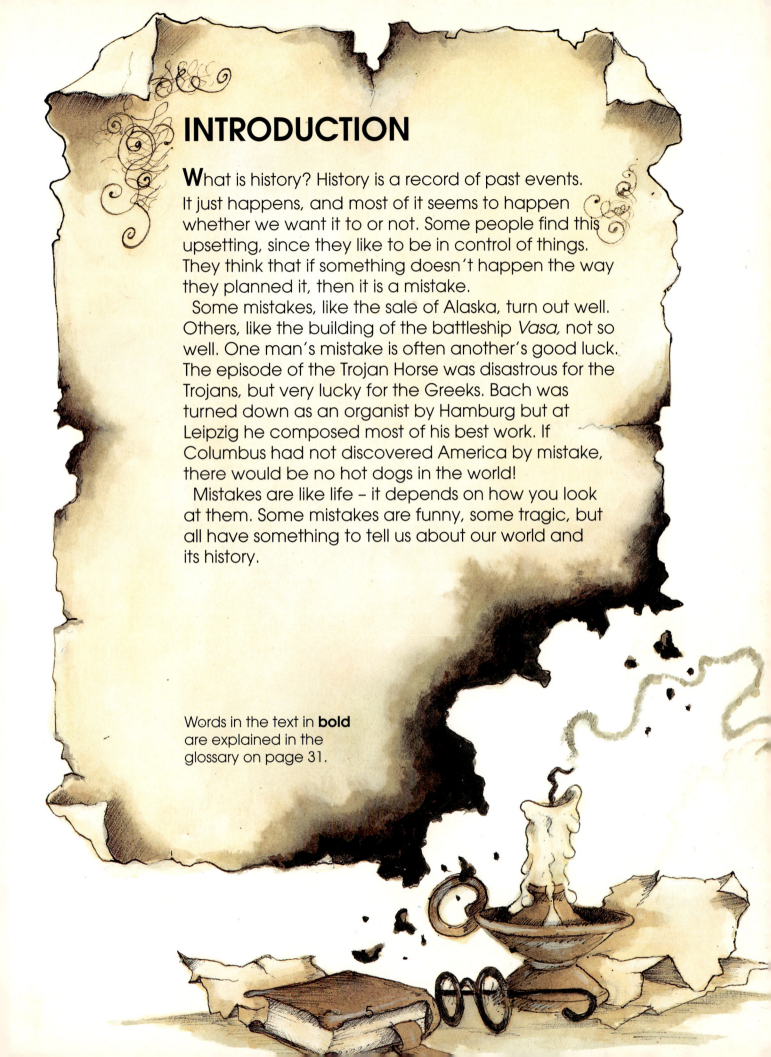

A Gun Too Many?

Gustavus Adolphus was one of Sweden's most powerful kings. A shrewd ruler and a mighty soldier, he made Sweden the most powerful of all the Baltic nations in the seventeenth century. There was, however, one episode in his reign which Gustavus would rather have left out of the history books. This was the disastrous sinking of his newest warship on its first and only voyage.

In 1625, Sweden was at war with Poland. Gustavus Adolphus decided to frighten his enemies by building a great warship, the biggest in the world. It was to be called the *Vasa*, which was the family name of the kings and queens of Sweden.

And so the Swedish **shipwrights** set to work. More than 1,000 oak trees were felled to make the hull. Whole pine trees formed the masts and yards, and over 1,000 square metres of cloth were used to make the sails. The ship carried 60 guns, which was more than any other warship afloat.

Why did the *Vasa* sink?

The Vasa capsized because she was top-heavy. She was built by highly-skilled men, but they had no way of predicting how the ship would behave with so many guns on board. You could say that the fault lay with Gustavus Adolphus. If he had been content with a few less guns this ship would have been more stable.

On 10 August 1628, the *Vasa* was ready to sail. All the people of Stockholm lined the harbour as the ship was towed into open water. Bands played, the crowd cheered, flags fluttered bravely, and deafening **salvoes** were fired from the *Vasa's* guns. Once clear of the harbour, the sails were set, and majestically the ship gathered speed.

Suddenly, a gust of wind **heeled** the ship over, and water began to pour into her open gunports. Within minutes she was awash, and the whole of Stockholm watched in horror and amazement as the *Vasa*, with sails still set and flags flying, sank beneath the waves.

Salvaged at last

For over 300 years the *Vasa* remained on the sea bed, and in time was completely forgotten. In 1956, the ship was rediscovered, and in 1961 she was raised, almost intact, to the surface. The *Vasa* is now preserved in a museum at Stockholm, a remarkable example of seventeenth century shipbuilding.

The Mary Rose

Gustavus Adolphus should have read his history books. In 1545, in England, the *Mary Rose*, flagship of King Henry VIII, sank in exactly the same way as the *Vasa* and for exactly the same reasons. The *Mary Rose* has been raised and is preserved in a museum in Portsmouth, England.

A FLIGHT OF FANCY

According to the myths of ancient Greece, there was once a famous inventor, called Daedalus. It was he who built the terrible **labyrinth** for Minos, King of Crete. In the labyrinth lurked the terrible Minotaur, a monster who was half man and half bull...but that's another story.

Despite making such a splendid job of the labyrinth, Daedalus fell out with King Minos. As a result, both Daedalus and his son, Icarus, were imprisoned at the top of a high mountain in Crete, from which there seemed to be no way down. But Minos had forgotten that Daedalus was a brilliant inventor, and soon he had devised a way of escaping from the king.

First Daedalus collected feathers from the birds that shared their lofty prison. Then, using the melted wax from their candles, he stuck the feathers together to make two pairs of wings. When they were finished, Daedalus and Icarus strapped on their wings. 'Whatever you do, Icarus,' warned Daedalus. 'Do not fly too high. If you fly too near the sun, the wax in your wings will melt.'

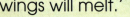

Together, father and son leapt from their prison window and flew out. They soared high over the mountains of Crete, and soon they were over the sea and on their way to Sicily.

Icarus began to enjoy himself. He started to show off, performing aerobatic stunts and flying upside-down. Then he decided to see how high he could fly. Ignoring his father's warning, he flew up and up, higher and higher, until he was a mere speck against the blazing light of the sun.

Just as his father had warned, the sun's heat began to melt the wax in his wings. One by one, the feathers dropped away. Too late, Icarus realized his mistake, but already the feathers were falling apart.

Before long Icarus' wings had completely disappeared. He plummeted headlong into the sea and was drowned.

What happened to Daedalus?

The body of poor Icarus was washed up on the Greek island which is now called Icaria, in his memory.

Daedalus flew on to Sicily, where he continued to invent things and lived to a ripe old age.

THE SALE OF THE CENTURY

When, in 1867, the American government bought Alaska from the Russians, most people thought it was a big mistake. The man who negotiated the deal was William H. Seward. He thought that at a price of $7,200,000 (under $5 a square kilometre) Alaska was too good to miss. Few of his fellow Americans agreed. After all, the country was nothing but high mountains, dense forests, and snow. For many years afterwards Alaska was known as 'Seward's Folly'.

Back in 1741, the Danish explorer, Vitus Bering, had landed in Alaska and claimed it for the Russian Tsar. But because it was so far from St Petersburg or Moscow, few Russians ever travelled there. Only a few hunters went in search of beaver, otter and bear skins, and they did not establish a permanent settlement until 1784. Alaska was more trouble than it was worth. Russia just did not need more mountains, forests or snow. So when William Seward asked to buy it, the Russian Tsar was happy to sell.

In the long run, Alaska has proved to be a brilliant investment. In 1897, gold was discovered at Klondike, and the famous Klondike **gold rush** began. Then other metals, such as chrome, copper, zinc, nickel, mercury and platinum, were soon found. But the most dramatic discovery of all was that of oil.

Alaska is no longer known as Seward's Folly and it seems that it was the Tsar of Russia, and not William Seward, who made the big mistake.

Facts and figures

In January 1959, Alaska became the forty-ninth state of the United States of America. Its area is 1,520,700 square kilometres, of which one third is within the Arctic Circle. Mount McKinley in Alaska is 6,194 metres high, which is higher than any other mountain in the United States. The population of Alaska is only 400,000 and 64,000 of these are Inuit or Eskimos. Alaska is Eskimo for 'Big Country'.

Who 'owned' Alaska?

Native American Indians and Eskimos have lived in Alaska for thousands of years. When Vitus Bering claimed Alaska for the Tsar, he didn't bother asking their permission. Nor did they get a single cent from the sale of 1867.

11

'LET THEM EAT CAKE'

In the winter of 1789 the government of France was bankrupt and its people were starving. The country's money had been spent on war, people in power were greedy and corrupt, and to cap it all the harvest had been the worst for years. Wheat had become very expensive, and in the capital city of Paris many poor people could not even afford to buy bread to eat.

Meanwhile, a few miles outside the city in the magnificent palace of Versailles, the Queen of France, Marie Antoinette, happily fed sweets and cake to her pet lambs. She knew little, and cared less, about the problems of her people, who gave the queen the nickname 'Madame **Deficit**' because she spent so much money. Many people believed that it was the queen's influence over her weak husband, King Louis XVI, that caused all the troubles in France.

When spring came the king and his advisers grew increasingly worried. The people of Paris were hungry and restless. Trouble was brewing.

'The people have no bread!' the king told the queen. 'No bread?' said the queen.
'*Then let them eat cake!*'

On 14 July 1789, the people of Paris rose in revolt and stormed the hated prison of the Bastille. In October they marched on Versailles and arrested the king and queen. Louis and Marie remained prisoners until 1791 when, foolishly, they tried to escape. As a result they were sentenced to death.

'*Let her eat cake!*' the crowd jeered as the queen climbed the steps to the guillotine. She must have wished she could have eaten her words.

A bloody end for bloodthirsty men

Many of the **revolutionaries** came to sticky ends as well. Robespierre and Danton, two of the leaders of the revolution, were both guillotined by their former comrades within a year of Marie Antoinette's death. They were condemned by laws that they had introduced. Marat, another revolutionary, was stabbed to death in his bath.

The guillotine

The guillotine was introduced to France by Dr Joseph Guillotin as a quick and foolproof method of execution. It was used by the revolutionary government to eliminate any suspected enemies of the Revolution. By 1794 more than 3,000 French men and women in Paris had lost their heads.

The Giant Dustbowl

Long ago, an endless sea of grass covered the high plains of mid-western America. Huge herds of buffalo grazed there, and these were hunted by the native Indians who wandered the plains following the migrations of their prey.

In the nineteenth century, white men decided to settle on this grassy land. They chased the Indians away and shot all the buffalo. The white settlers divided the land into ranches and introduced European cattle to breed and grow fat on the juicy grass. In time, the cattle ate all the grass and they grew weak and thin.So the settlers began to think of some other way of using the land.

In the 1920s, the price of wheat in America rose sharply. The settlers of the High Plains decided that they could make more money by growing wheat, instead of raising cattle. So they became farmers. They ploughed up the land and planted field upon field of wheat.

For a few years all was well. Then, in 1933, the rain did not fall as usual. In fact, it scarcely rained for the next five years. The crops failed from lack of water, and the land became as dry as a bone. The top soil which had once been so rich turned to dust.

Because the crops had died and there was no grass left, there were no roots in the earth to hold the soil together. Large parts of Colorado, Kansas, Texas and Oklahoma were turned into a giant 'dustbowl'. High winds whipped up the dust into great clouds. These created black blizzards up to eight kilometres high. The blizzards were so thick that the sun was blotted out and day turned into night.

The farms became desert and by 1939 most people had moved out. The farmers had been ruined by their own cattle, their own ploughs and their own greed.

Repeated mistake

In the 1940s, the US government began a replanting programme to reclaim the 'dustbowl'. They planted grass to bind the soil and stop it blowing away. Gradually, farmers were able to return. Despite this experience, people all over the world are still making the same mistake of over-grazing and over-cultivation.

BUILDING BLUNDERS

The Tacoma Narrows Bridge

In 1940, an enormous suspension bridge was built across the Puget Sound, an inlet of the sea in Washington State, USA. The bridge soon earned the nickname 'Galloping Gertie' because in bad weather the huge, 850-metre span of metal writhed and heaved in a terrifying way. One day, only four months after it was built, there was a fierce wind. Galloping Gertie trembled and shook so much that, with an almighty crash, the whole bridge collapsed and fell into the waters below.

Fonthill Abbey

In 1796, an eccentric English millionaire, called William Beckford, began to build a house in the style of a medieval abbey. James Wyatt, the architect, was a man of good reputation and much experience. Unfortunately, the builder was not quite as reliable. He failed to make the foundations of the abbey strong enough to support the giant tower built at its centre. One dark night, in 1807, the enormous central tower caved in. The abbey was so big that Beckford, asleep in one of the wings, was unaware of the disaster until told by his servants the next morning.

The City of Emperor Abu Akbar

In 1569, Emperor Abu Akbar decided to build a grand new capital city at a place called Fatehpur Sikri near Agra, in India. Finally, in 1574, the magnificent city was finished. Akbar was delighted and moved his entire court there.

But 14 years later Fatehpur Sikri was abandoned. Nobody could live there. It seems that the water supply was not adequate, and even emperors have to wash!

The Pyramid at Meidum

The ancient Eygptians were famous for their feats of engineering, but even they had their off-days. At a place called Meidum, they built a vast pyramid, more than 140 metres high, as a tomb for one of their pharaohs. Unfortunately the sides of the pyramid were made so steep that they became unstable. One day, as the army of slaves toiled and sweated to finish the pyramid, there was a strange rumbling noise. Suddenly an enormous avalanche of stones hurtled down, crushing the thousands of people working below. With a thunderous crash, the entire structure collapsed. This disaster is probably the worst architectural catastrophe in history.

RAVENOUS RABBITS

In 1770 Captain James Cook, an Englishman, became the first European to set foot in Australia. He discovered a continent full of wonderful new sights. The forests of eucalyptus trees, deserts and grasslands were inhabited by many animals Cook had never seen before. There were emus, kangaroos, wallabies and koalas. But in the whole continent there was not one single rabbit.

Unfortunately, wherever English people settled, rabbits went along too. So, in the nineteenth century, English colonists transported rabbits with them to Australia. Inevitably, some of the rabbits escaped into the **outback**. The rabbits took to their new home straight away. There was plenty of grass and other juicy plants to eat, few predators and millions of empty Australian acres in which to dig burrows. Rabbits breed very quickly, so before long there were many more rabbits than people.

By the 1880s these harmless little creatures were becoming a serious menace. In some areas the rabbits ate all the crops, so that farmers were ruined. In others they ate all the grass, so that the land turned to desert. The rabbit warrens became so large and numerous that in some places the earth collapsed into deep ravines.

The Australian people did everything they could to reduce the rabbit population. Hunters shot them or trapped them, but the rabbits continued to multiply. Everyone grew tired of eating roast rabbit, grilled rabbit, rabbit stew and rabbit pie.

So, in the 1950s, the government decided to introduce a terrible disease, called myxomatosis, into the rabbit population. The disease was fatal, and millions of rabbits died. At last, it seemed the rabbit problem was solved. Gradually, however, the surviving rabbits bred and multiplied, and even now, all over Australia, they are burrowing away.

Dummy bunnies
One idea for reducing the rabbit population was to put life-sized dummy male rabbits into the rabbit warrens. The dummy males would scare off the live male rabbits, but attract the females to stay in the warren. Once the males and females were separated they could not breed.

JOURNEY

Not all mistakes end badly. Christopher Columbus' big mistake resulted in the discovery of two new continents and changed the course of history.

Christopher Columbus (or Cristobal Colon as he preferred to be called) was born in 1451, in Genoa, Italy. This was a time of great sea voyages, when European explorers sailed to India, China and Japan by travelling round the tip of Africa. The journey was long and dangerous and sometimes took up to two years. Columbus was sure there was an easier way of sailing to the countries in the east. He knew that the world was round. So, he thought, instead of going east across the Indian Ocean, why not go west across the Atlantic?

How America got its name

In 1507 the new continents were named America, after Amerigo Vespucci, an Italian explorer who sailed to South America a few years after Columbus.

To the Edge

Columbus went to the King of Portugal and explained his plan to find a new route to the lands known as the **Indies.** The king was not impressed. In fact he told Columbus that if he sailed west instead of east he would undoubtedly sail off the edge of the world. Columbus, however, was not going to give up that easily. He went off to see King Ferdinand and Queen Isabella of Spain. They, too, were doubtful, and for four years Columbus waited for their decision to help him. 'Trust me, your majesties,' said Columbus.

'My calculations show that the Indies are to the west of Spain.'

Eventually, Queen Isabella gave Columbus money to equip his expedition. So, in August 1492, Columbus sailed from Spain with three ships, *Santa Maria, Pinta* and *Nina.* At last, after many weeks at sea, on 12 October 1492, there was a shout from the look-out. 'Land ahoy!'

Columbus and his crew were overjoyed. They thought they had reached the Indies, which are islands in the east.

In fact, Columbus had really sighted the Bahamas, islands in the west. Without knowing it, he had discovered America! Columbus went on to land on Cuba and Hispaniola, and finally, before he died, he found the mainland of central America. His voyages of discovery were the beginning of a new and momentous era in world history.

The Indians of America
The islands discovered by Columbus were populated. Because he thought he had landed in the Indies, Columbus called the people 'Indians'. Today, the islands of the Caribbean are known as the West Indies.

THE VALLEY OF DEATH

The Crimean War lasted from 1854 to 1856. France, Turkey and Britain fought on one side, against Russia on the other. In this war there were many military blunders, but by far the most spectacular was the Charge of the Light Brigade.

   The commander of the Light Brigade was Lord Cardigan, a man more famous for his whiskers than his military skill. On 25 October 1854, while the Battle of Balaclava was raging, the Light Brigade was ordered to stop the Russians hauling away some cannon they had just captured.

   The man who gave the order was Lord Lucan, the British Commander-in-Chief. The soldier who delivered the order to Lord Cardigan was a junior officer, called Captain Nolan.

'Commander-in-chief's compliments, sir,' said Nolan. 'Will you please stop the Russians removing the guns.'

'Guns, sir?' snapped Lord Cardigan.

       'Which guns?'

Lord Cardigan

Captain Nolan

Lord Lucan

Captain Nolan gazed uncertainly at the Russian lines. There were guns everywhere. Which guns had Lord Lucan meant? The young captain pointed down to the end of the valley.
'There, sir,' said Nolan. 'There are your guns!'
Lord Cardigan stared in disbelief. Ranged on the hills on either side of the valley were Russian troops, with guns loaded and ready to fire. But orders were orders, and he must do as he was commanded. Lord Cardigan turned to his men.
'Forward the Light Brigade!' he roared. 'Charge!'
  The five regiments of highly-trained soldiers did not question the orders of their leader. They bravely rode straight down the valley towards the guns at the other end.
  The Russians were amazed at this folly and fired their cannon as fast as they could. Hundreds of British soldiers and horses fell to the ground. Amazingly, Lord Cardigan reached the end of the valley unharmed, but when he turned to rally his men the awful truth was clear. The Light Brigade was shot to pieces. They had attacked the wrong guns.

23

BACH'S FAILED AUDITION

In the early eighteenth century the **elders** of the Church of St James in Hamburg were faced with such a choice. Sadly, they made the wrong one.

In 1720 a new organist was needed for the church. By coincidence, Johann Sebastian Bach was visiting Hamburg at this time. Bach was a brilliant musician, both a player and a composer of organ music. While in Hamburg he performed several concerts, and astonished everyone with his musical genius. Many people in Hamburg thought it would be a great privilege to have such a man playing regularly in their church.

Bach had to leave Hamburg for a while, but he told the church elders that he would take the job of organist if they were to offer it to him.

Nevertheless, the elders decided to hold a musical competition. The candidates played through their chosen pieces. Compared to Bach, their playing sounded very amateur. It was obvious to everyone that the elders should ask Bach to return and take the job. For a month the elders' decision was kept secret. Finally, in December 1720, the new organist was announced. His name was Johann...Joachim Heitmann!

Why had the elders chosen him? It was very puzzling. A few weeks later, all became clear.

Heitmann had little taste or talent, but he did have a lot of money. After his election he paid four thousand marks to the coffers of St James Church. As for Bach, he eventually went to Leipzig, where he achieved lasting fame as the greatest organist and composer of his age.

Johann Sebastian Bach

Bach was born at Eisenach, in Germany, in 1685. At the age of ten he went to live with his elder brother at Ohrdruf. There he became a chorister, and studied the organ and klavier. In 1708, at the age of 23, Bach became organist to the Duke of Saxe-Weimar, then, in 1717, to the Prince of Anhalt-Cothen. Having been turned down by Hamburg, in 1723 Bach went to St Thomas' Church in Leipzig. There, until his death in 1750, Bach composed hundreds of musical works.

THE WOODEN HORSE

The story of the Trojan horse begins in Greece about 3,000 years ago when Paris, Prince of Troy, fell in love with Helen, the wife of King Menelaus of Sparta. While Menelaus was away on business, Paris ran off with Helen and took her to his **citadel** at Troy.

When King Menelaus heard the news he was furious. He quickly met his brother, Agamemnon, King of the Greeks.

'Helen must be brought back!' raged Menelaus.

'Then we will lay siege to Troy,' said his brother.

Together they assembled an army and sailed to Troy. For ten years the Greeks besieged the mighty city, but without success. At last Odysseus, the most cunning of the Greek captains, devised a plan.

Paris   Menelaus and Helen

Soon the Trojans were very relieved to see the Greeks board their ships and sail away. Imagine their surprise when they saw a great wooden horse standing in front of the city walls. How had it got there? What was it for? A Greek named Sinon, pretended to be a deserter, and told the Trojans that the horse was a present dedicated to the goddess Athena.
'It will protect your city from all your enemies,' he said.

So the Trojans dragged the huge wooden horse inside the walls. A wise old Trojan, called Laocoon, warned the citizens against doing this. 'You're making a big mistake!' said the old man. 'It could be a trick.' But, alas, nobody listened.

That night, while the people of Troy celebrated, the Greek fleet sailed quietly back in the darkness. Sinon, the Greek, crept up to the wooden horse and opened a secret door in its belly. Out jumped King Menelaus and his men, who were hidden inside. They opened the city gates and let in the waiting Greek army, who rushed in, reclaimed Helen and burned the city of Troy to the ground.

Fact or fiction?
The story of the fall of Troy was told by the Greek poet Homer in his poem the *Iliad*. This was composed about 800 BC, and over the centuries has become regarded more as legend than fact. In 1870, the German archaeologist Heinrich Schliemann discovered the ruins of an ancient city at Hisarlik on the coast of Turkey. Its position fitted exactly the description of Troy given by Homer, and it was discovered that this city had been destroyed by fire around 1200 BC. Could this be the ancient capital of the Trojans?

Troy's revenge
One Trojan, named Aeneas, escaped from Troy. After many adventures he landed in Italy, and founded a city. The descendants of Aeneas were the Romans, and their empire included not only Italy, but Troy, Greece and the entire Mediterranean world.

SPLITTING THE ATOM

It was Albert Einstein who first suggested that a single particle of matter – an **atom** – might contain an enormous quantity of energy. In the first half of the twentieth century, scientists of many countries raced to be the first to split the atom, in order to unleash the this amazing source of power. Atomic power could provide heat and light in every home.

In 1911, an English scientist, Sir Ernest Rutherford, first discovered the structure of atoms.

Then, in 1938, two Germans, Otto Hahn and Fritz Strassmann, first split the atom by firing neutrons at the nucleus. They discovered that when the nucleus splits it gives off energy.

Finally, in 1942, an Italian, Enrico Fermi showed how the power released by the atom could be controlled and used by man. If the power is controlled it can produce light and heat for our homes. But if it is not controlled it produces an explosion.

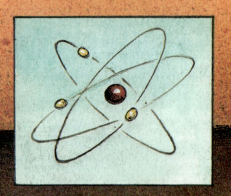

The nucleus, or centre of the atom, is circled by a number of fast-moving electrons.

When the nucleus splits it gives off energy.

Nuclear power has now become a vital source of energy and many countries have developed atomic power stations to generate electricity for peaceful purposes.

Unfortunately the same power has also become a way of creating bombs capable of terrible destruction. Today, there are enough nuclear weapons in the world to destroy our planet. What would Albert Einstein have thought of all this? Until his death in 1955 he was a **pacifist**, horrified at the way atomic power was being used. Einstein may have thought that splitting the atom was the biggest mistake of all.

TIME LINE

Time Line	Event Date	Event
	c 2590 BC	The Pyramid at Meidum
1100 BC	c 2000 BC	Daedalus and Icarus
1000 BC	c 1200 BC	The Trojan Horse
BC		
Birth of Christ		
1000 AD		
1400	1492	Christopher Columbus
1500	1569	Fatehpur Sikri
1600	1628	The Vasa
1700	1720	J S Bach
	1770	Discovery of Australia
	1789	Marie Antoinette
1800	1807	Fonthill Abbey
	1854	The Charge of the Light Brigade
	1867	The Sale of Alaska
1900	1933	The Giant Dustbowl
	1938	Splitting the Atom
	1940	The Tacoma Narrows Bridge

GLOSSARY

atom: the smallest particle of individual matter.

citadel: a stronghold or fortress.

deficit: you get this when you
spend more money than you earn.

elders: a name given to the officials in some churches.

gold rush: a rush of people hurrying to a part
of the world where gold has been discovered
hoping to get rich quickly.

heeled: leaning over with the force of the wind.

Indies: an old European name for the east,
particularly India and south-east Asia.

labyrinth: the ancient Greek word given to
the maze which Daedalus constructed for
King Minos. It is now used to describe any
system of confusing tunnels or a place where
it is easy to get lost.

outback: the Australian name for uncultivated
countryside or wilderness.

pacifist : someone who believes in solving disputes
by peaceful rather than violent means.

revolutionary: someone who wants to change how a
country is run, often by violent methods.
When this happens it is called a **revolution.**

salvo: this is when many guns fire at the same time,
often as a salute or celebration.

shipwright: a builder of wooden ships. Wright is an
old-fashioned word for craftsman or builder.

INDEX